UNCONVENTIONAL
Wisdom

Conversations with Legends

WISDOM MARTIN

Unconventional Wisdom: Conversations with Legends. Copyright 2024 by Wisdom Martin.

All rights reserved. No part of this publication may be reproduced, distributed, or transmitted in any form or by any means, including photocopying, recording, or other electronic or mechanical methods, without the prior written permission of the publisher, except in the case of brief quotations embodied in critical reviews and certain other noncommercial uses permitted by copyright law.

For permission requests, write to the publisher, addressed "Attention: Permissions Coordinator," 205 N. Michigan Avenue, Suite #810, Chicago, IL 60601. 13th & Joan books may be purchased for educational, business or sales promotional use. For information, please email the Sales Department at sales@13thandjoan.com.

Printed in the U. S. A.

First Printing, February 2025

Library of Congress Cataloging-in-Publication Data has been applied for.

ISBN: 978-1-7335154-2-9

DEDICATION

With love to my late father Wisdom Martin, the greatest man I have ever known.

My mother Shirley Beamon Martin, the greatest woman I have ever known!

CONTENTS

Foreword vii
Introduction ix

Chapter 1.   Becoming Number 1: Caleb Williams 1
Chapter 2.   Do you Believe in Magic: Magic Johnson 13
Chapter 3.   Design your path: Ruth E. Carter 23
Chapter 4.   Talent & Taps: Gregory Hines 31
Chapter 5.   Basketball to Business: Shaq 41
Chapter 6.   Playing with Prince: Prince's Band
                   The Revolution 49
Chapter 7.   Marvelous: the Russo Brothers 59
Chapter 8.   Pitch Perfect: Leslie Jordan 67
Chapter 9.   New Edition's New Addition: Ralph Tresvant &
                   Johnny Gill 73
Chapter 10. One Night in College Park: The Texas
                   Western Game 81

Chapter 11. Air Jordan's Last Flight:
           A Moment With Jordan......................87
Chapter 12. Reality: Nene Leakes 93

About The Author..................................... 101

FOREWORD

Greatness occurs when grit and drive encounter opportunity. Countless talents abound, yet without the right timing and circumstances, achieving greatness may be delayed. While some paths are clear and direct, others are more complex. A consistent factor in any victory is the determination to cross the finish line.

Unconventional Wisdom offers a rare opportunity to journey alongside legends as they pursue greatness, with their unique perspective serving as our guiding light. Everyone has a testimony of how they arrived at their destination. When they allow us a glimpse of their story, they let us in on their proudest moments as well as their greatest setbacks. Each story gives us an intimate view of how those we admire accepted the challenge of greatness. Unconventional Wisdom teaches lessons that may impact our choices when our opportunity for greatness arrives.

Gaining a deeper insight into the origins of greatness provides us with what we truly desire: Unconditional Wisdom.

BARAKA W. PEREZ, PhD,
Medical Psychologist

INTRODUCTION

All readers should be able to read the interviews with gratitude and grasp the outstanding information that each person provided. If only for a moment, anyone who reads the information should be able to discern the importance of it. The purpose of this information is to illustrate that struggles and challenges are universal and not exclusive to any particular life experience. It is hoped that readers may discover valuable thoughts and insights that could positively impact their lives.

It is quite clear that the people interviewed were diligent, serious and truthful about the information they imparted. Their sharp level of intelligence, thoroughness, and dedication was to provide knowledge that would be helpful and lasting for anyone who reads the interviews.

If you can open your mind and envision their struggles, perhaps this will cause you to learn and grow in a positive direction. Anyone who carefully reads the interviews should stop and think about their life and realize that there is much to be gained from reading the interviews. I found that all the information could be a wonderful way to find the truth about your life and strive for solace when you have a struggle or a bump in the road. Acknowledging a struggle or a road bump could make you physically and mentally stronger. No one is immune to hardships. Struggles are not limited to certain people, certain lifestyles, or certain geographical locations. Anyone has the ability to tap into the magic within themselves, whether it's to determine the necessity for a new edition in their own life or to embrace authenticity and join a new revolution for self-improvement.

Chapter 1

BECOMING NUMBER 1: CALEB WILLIAMS

"Make sure you love what you do every day. You should be able to wake up before your alarm and love what you are doing."

Caleb Williams-Heisman Trophy Winner 2022

Long before Caleb Williams became the top pick for the Chicago Bears or put on a football uniform as a kid and started throwing passes, he and his family were on a path to success.

If you think about all the things it takes to be a successful college athlete, it is mind boggling. The hard work, the confidence, the swagger, the intelligence and the support system. You must be in the best situation with your school, the coaches, and the team. Everything must fall in place for you to succeed and keep succeeding. If one thing is off it could derail the entire career at any point. In life, things don't always go according to plans. So what happens when you have to pivot or make a huge adjustment?

When Caleb Williams walked into the room for our conversation, he exuded confidence and the poise of a young man well beyond his age. You could tell he was built for the moment and ready for the NFL.

As a high school football phenom, Caleb Williams rose to prominence at Gonzaga College High School in Washington D.C. He was one of the top quarterback recruits in the country. He decided to go to Oklahoma to play for coach Lincoln Riley. Riley had a track record for developing quarterbacks for the NFL.

In the 2022 college football season, quarterback Caleb Williams transferred from Oklahoma to USC. His coach, Lincoln Riley, the man who recruited him to Oklahoma, had taken a new coaching job at USC? Yes, he had been a highly touted recruit out of Washington, D.C.'s Gonzaga High. Yes, he had some success at Oklahoma when he replaced the entrenched starter, Spencer Rattler. But nobody knew what was about to happen once Caleb Williams stormed the field for the Trojans.

"I started playing football around 4 years old. I loved it. I played all the other sports. After exploring various sports, I consistently found myself returning to football. I actually realized around 10 years old that's when I made the decision to switch to quarterback. I told my dad this is what I want to do for the rest of my life. Be a quarterback, spread the ball around, and go win big games."

Off the field, Williams says the transition from being a high school star to a college star was not difficult.

"College was not very challenging and a lot of that comes from Gonzaga College High School. Gonzaga was very challenging. The time you're there in class is like oh my god. But it all paid off. You get to college; you have the experience you get to have. Living in D.C., one of the best cities if not the best city in the world. I get to move around LA. I came from D.C., where there are lots of personalities and people of all races and religions. It kind of prepared me for the big city of LA."

He was the #1 rated quarterback in high school, and had committed to Oklahoma to play for Coach Lincoln Riley. The challenge was, he was going to back up Spencer Rattler who was a top prospect in 2019. Rattler was a Heisman favorite coming into the season.

Williams remained on the bench until Oklahoma played its rival Texas. Spencer Rattler was struggling and had 2 turnovers with the Sooners, trailing 35-17. Coach Riley pulled Rattler and replaced him with Williams. Caleb fueled a furious comeback with Oklahoma winning 55-48.

"I went to Oklahoma with a quarterback ahead of me that had all the accolades. I went there, competed, and worked hard. Coach Riley decided to put me on the field because he had faith in my abilities and trusted me, despite my young age of 18 at the time."

The next week, Williams started his first game against TCU completing 18 of 23 passes for 295 yards, with 4 touchdown passes and 1 rushing touchdown. Oklahoma won 52-31. He was the first true freshman starter at Oklahoma since 1999.

Against Texas Tech, Williams threw for 400 yards and a record 6 touchdown passes.

He concluded his freshman season in the 2021 Alamo Bowl against Oregon, completing 21 of 27 for 242 yards in Oklahoma's 47-32 win.

In a surprising offseason decision, Coach Lincoln Riley accepted a position at USC, prompting Williams to follow him to the West Coast.

"Going to LA, I was prepared for the moment. I had all my goals in mind. I couldn't wait to go on the big stage and go out there and perform," Williams said.

It was one of the best statistical seasons for a quarterback in USC history. Williams set a single season record for total offense (4,919 yards), most touchdown passes (42), completions (333), passing yards (4537), and passing efficiency rating (168.5). His 322 rushing yards marked the highest total by a USC quarterback in 70 years. He earned unanimous first-team All-American honors and secured the 2022 Heisman Trophy. He was the 7th USC player to win the award. Now comes the next challenge, trying to improve on what was a historic first year. How does someone so young deal with the pressure of being on top of the college football world?

"I wasn't surprised at all. Maybe on the first run. I was a bit angry when I went out on the field. I felt like I should have been playing. I used that to motivate me. So when I got out there, I broke loose and I looked around a little bit, that was the only part I was surprised about. Nobody was in front of me. I just had to run. I actually went out there like I was going to score once I got the ball in my hands. I stick to my routine. I don't worry about anybody's expectations, pressure, or anything like that. I didn't think pressure is a thing if you are prepared. During the offseason, one must prepare both mentally and physically for those crucial moments everyone dreams of – the shots, the opportunities for glory, like executing a two-minute drive to win the game. You prepare for those moments. I don't look at any expectations and pressure other than me and my team. This year, it's the top of the food chain for us."

Caleb says none of this would even be possible if it wasn't for the tremendous support of his family. "Whether it's putting the right people in my life, the trainers, putting me on the right team, the right people, the right coaches helping me with the progress. Whether that's in football, or in life, they have been tremendous."

Yes, the family created the environment, but Williams had to do his part and put in the work.

"A lot of it comes from preparation and hard work. Also, the relationship with my coach, Lincoln Riley, over the past few years. It's the best it's ever been. That's a big part of it. Just believing in myself."

Sports are constantly changing and evolving. From the time Williams left Gonzaga College High School for college, the rules changed, allowing college athletes to make money from Name Image and Likeness deals (NIL). Essentially, college athletes could now make money from commercials and endorsements, among other things.

"It changed the landscape of college. I love it. I get to do something I've always wanted to do as a kid, which is be independent, pay my own bills, and don't have to worry about calling Dad asking for money. I was in college before NIL. I've been on both sides of it. I also get to help other people and give back to my teammates, build relationships." In 2023, Williams was one of college football's top 5 NIL athletes earning more than 2 million dollars in endorsements. He was prominently featured in commercials for Dr. Pepper, Wendy's, and Nissan.

Being the top player in college football came with lots of other perks. Williams was at the 2023 Super Bowl between Kansas City and Philadelphia. The NFL's most significant game was historic as it marked the first time two black quarterbacks, Patrick Mahomes and Jaylen Hurts, competed against each other for the championship.

"I was really excited to see 2 good teams, 2 good quarterbacks facing off. I've known Jaylen Hurts. I've watched Patrick Mahomes a lot. In the game, whether it's mentally or physically, I see a good amount of me when I watch them. I was watching the game from a different perspective. It was cool to see Rihanna at halftime. It was pretty awesome to see how the game has progressed," Williams recalled.

The fact Williams was seeing quarterbacks that looked like him on both teams in the NFL's biggest game was a story within itself. Williams was already drawing comparisons to NFL 2-time MVP and 3-time champion Patrick Mahomes by the way he played. Williams was following in his footsteps and the path of all the other African-American quarterbacks before him. I told the story of the black quarterback in my 2022 book, *"Pass Interference: The History of the Black Quarterback in the NFL."*

Throughout his journey, Caleb Williams has been remarkably resilient.

Expectations were high for USC in his junior year. The Trojans had a rough season finishing 7-5 after starting 6-0. While the team defense took a huge step backwards, Caleb was brilliant on offense and solidified his future as the top pick in the 2024 NFL draft. He's been able to navigate the ups and downs of football and success. For anyone out there who has ambitions on dealing with challenges of life, Williams has some advice.

"Whenever you are ready to make this not a dream but reality, whether you want to be the best real estate developer or best quarterback or whatever, get on a plan and find a routine. Make sure you love what you do every day. You should be able to wake up before your alarm and love what you are doing."

Chapter 2

DO YOU BELIEVE IN MAGIC: MAGIC JOHNSON

"I have been living with this disease and I look just like you."

Magic Johnson-NBA Hall of famer

Magic with my championship Hoops for Homeless team.

Nobody could do what Magic Johnson could do. Basketball had never had a 6'9," ball handling, flashy point guard with a giant smile and an even bigger personality. He was just a big, agile, player. He was a leader. He was a winner. He won in high school, he won the 1979 NCAA Championship at Michigan State, he was the first pick in the draft by the LA Lakers, and as a rookie, led them to the NBA championship in 1980 winning finals MVP. He was the orchestrator of "Showtime" Lakers basketball and the Lakers Fast Break in the 80s. He made passing cool. Over the next 10 years, Magic led the LA Lakers to 5 championships and won 3 MVP awards. He won an Olympic gold medal with the 1993 NBA Dream Team, which many say is the greatest basketball team ever assembled.

I remember November 7, 1991. I was at work when one of my coworkers came into the room with a sense of urgency. He yells out to me, "Your boy, Magic Johnson, just retired from the NBA after announcing he was HIV positive." At first, I believed he was joking, playing a cruel and not-so-funny joke. So, I ran to the television to see if what he was saying was true. Magic Johnson was holding a press conference with Kareem Abdul Jabbar and NBA Commissioner, David Stern, by his side explaining he was HIV positive. Like the rest of the world, I was shocked and stunned. Back then, this was considered, for the most part, a death sentence. It was sad and emotional to watch this basketball icon say he had to leave the game he revolutionized.

Before concluding his press conference, Magic informed the media audience that he was determined to overcome his situation. However, few people believed his statement. Magic never gave up. He came back to the NBA several times. He coached the Lakers for a short period. He thrived in the business world. He was investing in the black community with his Starbucks and movie franchises.

The first time I met Magic Johnson was after his announcement in the spring of 1992. Jackson State basketball star Lindsey Hunter had been drafted by the Detroit Pistons. Hunter hosted an all-star game at Jackson State, featuring none other than Hall of Famer Magic Johnson. I was working at WAPT news at the time as a cameraman. He did a live interview with the station, so I was responsible for putting the microphone on him and framing up the camera for the shot. The crowd was screaming in excitement. I spoke, "What's up Magic!" then shook his hand. "What's up man!" he responded with the trademark Magic Johnson smile. As I was fumbling putting the mic on him, we chatted for a hot second about how he would sneak in and out of Mississippi because his grandfather was from there. I was stunned that a 6 foot 9 basketball player named Magic could sneak anywhere.

Sixteen years later, I got a chance to see Magic Johnson again in Washington, D.C. Not only was he thriving and successfully living with HIV, but he was thriving in the business world. He invested millions in the black community with Starbucks franchises and movie franchises all over the country. His net worth was well over 600 million dollars.

As always, Magic was triumphant, approaching life with the same fervor he displayed on the basketball court. He also made it his business to be an advocate for HIV and safe sex.

I talked to him this time as a reporter about his HIV/AIDS campaign "I stand with Magic." "People, when it was first announced, thought I wasn't going to be here 16 years later. It's important that I am here to carry the message to different people," Magic said.

I met Magic at Howard University this time where he was educating the students and community leaders about his journey and being safe.

William Brawner, who at the time, was both a graduate of Howard University and HIV positive said, "As strong as the stigma is, HIV positive people who really care about this thing have to be able to show their face and say 'I have been living with this disease and I look just like you.' They never believe me because I look healthy."

Magic's message was out of concern that people were not listening to the warnings about safe sex and being tested.

"We need more and more people here in the D.C. area to be practicing safe sex. We know there is a major problem here," Magic said.

Statistics from Abbott HealthCare show at the end of 2006, Washington, D.C. had the highest rate of reported new aids cases nationwide. The mortality rate was nearly 10 times the national rate. "You can't have these type of numbers that we have in D.C. and not think that we don't have a long way to go," Magic said. "Early detection of this disease is important. There are almost 30 drugs now that can take care of people. Please, I am urging everybody to go out and get tested. Go back for your results. Know your status," Magic said.

In the first 2 years of the "I Stand With Magic Program" there were 460 testing events and 40,000 HIV tests donated.

"We need to make sure that we get people tested, go back for their results and understand it is a major problem," Magic said. "I understand a lot of times in this city people think it can't happen to them. A lot of the cases people are finding out late that they have either HIV or AIDS so that means they are really not going out and getting tested. God has been blessing me and my medicine has been working. We need more and more people here in the D.C. area to be practicing safe sex. We know that there is a major problem here. The person may look healthy, may look strong, but they can still be carrying the virus around."

Magic says the challenge is to educate and inform the impacted communities any way possible. "It's going to take us, the pastors, educators, health care providers; it's going to take everybody coming together. We have been lacking, whether it's information, whether it's testing, whatever it is, we need to get better at it so we can bring these numbers down. I have been able to prove you can go on and live a productive life. I think that's the other message I need to send to people." Year after year, Magic Johnson continues to be an advocate for AIDS awareness. He is a sports legend and the ultimate winner on and off the court. Magic has always thrived in the business world with that same winning attitude and approach that made him one of the greatest basketball players of all time.

By the end of 2023, Magic Johnson the businessman, was banking big bucks in the boardrooms of corporate America. According to Forbes, Magic's net worth was 1.2 billion dollars. He made 40 million playing in the NBA with the Lakers. His future finances were even more dynamic than the Lakers fast breaks he used to run. Magic Johnson's business empire includes ownership of movie theaters, Starbucks franchises, as well as ownership stakes in various sports teams such as the LA Dodgers (since 2012), LA Sparks (since 2014), LA FC (since 2018), and in 2023, he joined the ownership team of the Washington Commanders.

In 2023, billionaire businessman, Josh Harris, personally called Magic during his bid to buy the NFL team to include him in the ownership group. "Who wouldn't want Magic Johnson as a partner? First of all, he is a great guy. Even for me, he speaks in a way that motivates me. He is a man of faith, a man that has got 5 rings in the NBA," Harris said. "So many rings he doesn't have enough fingers. Obviously he comes from a different place than I do. He's an example. The league needs more people of color. He is really important to us. I'm glad he is here, he's really helping us."

In July, Harris and his team completed the purchase of the NFL franchise for a record 6 billion dollars.

"There is no bigger sports league than the NFL. It's been hard for us to get into the league," Magic said during a stop in D.C. Johnson and Harris had actually put a bid together to buy the Denver Broncos. That team was sold in 2022 to Walmart owner, Rob Walton, for 4.6 billion dollars.

When Washington was up for sale, this time Harris and Magic were able to complete the purchase. "I think the NFL is better because I'm standing here. I think the ownership group is better, we have a great leader in Josh who understands that as well," Magic said. "I know that there are a lot of minorities standing on my shoulders. But I have broad shoulders, that's why I am 6'9. I can handle that."

At 63 years old, Magic is living proof of overcoming the odds, succeeding, and living your best life no matter the circumstances.

Chapter 3

DESIGN YOUR PATH: RUTH E. CARTER

"Spike Lee was the first person to say 'Ruth Carter is our designer.' And it was because of 40 Acres and a Mule that I got the opportunity that I got."

Ruth E. Carter-Academy Award Winner

Ruth E. Carter didn't set out to be a professional costume designer. In fact, when she went to Hampton University they didn't even have a costume design program or curriculum. So how did she go from there to winning an Academy Award for the movie *Black Panther*?

"Hampton groomed me to follow my dreams. It encouraged me to light a fire and be the first," Carter said. With no curriculum for costume design in place, she had to, in her own words, 'design a path' where there was none. "I was able to create my own curriculum by doing all of the plays…it's a wonderful experience. It's a shared experience. We sometimes had these theater festivals where all these colleges would come together. It became a community. It really is a storytelling medium."

On campus, Carter poured her heart and soul into everything the theater had to offer. Creating outfits inside her room or wherever it was possible. Like those willing to sacrifice for success, she missed a lot of holidays and birthdays and family days because there was work that needed to be done in the theater.

Then came the big break with an encounter with another HBCU graduate from Morehouse College, Spike Lee.

"I was working in theatre. I was doing a dance company. He came and said, 'This is how you get more experience in film. Go to USC or UCLA and sign up to be on a student film,' and I did. I was on the weekends on a student film," Carter recalled. "Then, he called me one morning very early. I was in Los Angeles, he was in New York. He said, 'This is the man of your dreams.' And I was like, 'Denzel Washington?' He was like, 'No, this is Spike Lee. I want you to do my first studio film, *School Daze*.'" Lee began carving his path in Hollywood with his second film, *School Daze* (1988), which delved into the complexities of a fictional black college campus and the conflicts within its fraternity system.

"My first film. Because I had gone to a HBCU, I knew the lay of the land. So it was the perfect first project for me."

That collaboration led Carter to work with Spike Lee on other notable films such as *Do the Right Thing* (1989), *Mo' Better Blues* (1990), and *Jungle Fever* (1991).

Perfect for her and a lot of other young people from HBCUs. Spike Lee's production company, 40 Acres and a Mule, had started recruiting lots of students from Hampton University to work on his films. "We were representing back then. 40 Acres and a Mule was all about putting the diversity behind the camera that was not present. It was also telling the stories the way we want to tell them, not the way Hollywood wanted us to tell them."

Her work on Spike Lee's films eventually caught the attention of other filmmakers. Carter collaborated with Steven Spielberg on *Amistad* (1997), worked on John Singleton's *Rosewood* (1997) and *Baby Boy* (2001), and also partnered with Ava DuVernay.

Carter's impressive filmography spans at least 70 movies, including notable works such as *What's Love Got to Do with It, The Butler, Marshall, Selma, Dolemite Is My Name,* and *Coming 2 America.*

In 2018, Carter was chosen to costume design for the new Marvel film, *Black Panther*. This was the motion picture based on the black comic book superhero King T'Challa, the Black Panther, played by Howard University alum Chadwick Bozeman. "I had never designed for a superhero," Carter said. Ryan Coogler invited me into Marvel Studios. You can't just walk into Marvel. You got to get your eye scanned. You need a Tony Stark passcode." Coogler had grown up watching Spike Lee movies. He told Carter how he went to see the *Malcolm X* movie with his family when he was a young boy. Ryan told her he remembered the costumes from the Spike Lee movie. "I feel like I had auditioned for *Black Panther* when he (Coogler) was a child. It impacted him. It made a difference. I realized I had something I could bring to him as a filmmaker. I could already create worlds around heroes like Malcolm X. It just put me at ease."

The costumes she designed for Marvel comic book adaptations brought to life the fictional African nation of Wakanda. Her creations seamlessly blended African traditions with cutting-edge superhero technology.

At the 91st Academy Awards, Carter made history by winning an Academy Award for Best Costume Design for the *Black Panther*. She was a two-time Academy Award-winning American film costume designer, making history as the first and only black woman to receive an Academy Award for costume design. Her remarkable work also earned Marvel Studios its first-ever Oscar recognition. For *Black Panther: Wakanda Forever,* she became the first Black woman to win multiple Academy Awards in any category and the first costume designer to win for the first film and its sequel.

"It was a lot of butterflies, but the first person I saw in the audience was Spike Lee. Even though I won for *Black Panther*, which wasn't a Spike Lee Joint, I remember being in Giza at the pyramids on a Spike Lee Joint for *Malcolm X*."

"Spike Lee was the first person to say 'Ruth Carter is our designer.' And it was because of 40 Acres and a Mule that I got the opportunity that I got."

"I went off the speech and I said, 'Thank you, Spike, for my start. I hope this makes you proud,' because it was because of him that I was on stage. It was the first thing that really poured through my heart."

The same way that HBCU alum, Spike Lee, put her on a path to the highest level of costume design, Carter now wants to share her journey and inspire the next generation of HBCU students.

"I was a HBCU student. I didn't have mentors in costume design. I had to create mentors from other mediums. I think it's important that now that I have blazed a trail, that I bring people into this trail of costume design or even just how we grew into making this industry more inclusive." Carter said, "I have a love for HBCUs. I do feel like mentorship is important. It warms my heart to be around students."

"I think breaking barriers and making history and us really being hailed for doing something big in the industry, I do feel like I need to be present so other students can see that they, too, can make history. We have a long legacy of greatness," Carter said. "You know we weren't hailed.

We were not praised. We didn't have enough support. Well, now that we do, and we are becoming first, it's important that we show up; show up for each other. That's what making history for me is. It's not only pulling up our ancestry and all of the great things they did and showing our greatness, but it's also encouraging the next generation of greatness. Because they can step into my footsteps, and stand where I stand and be great."

Chapter 4

TALENT & TAPS: GREGORY HINES

"I think the most difficult thing is unemployment, so acting, singing, dancing or whatever, is why I wanted to be versatile."

Gregory Hines-Tap Dancer/Actor

Even if you're not familiar with the art of tap dancing, Gregory Hines was the epitome of brilliance in this genre. His footwork on stage was unparalleled. Not only was he the most talented tap dancer I had ever witnessed, but he also excelled as an actor, singer, and all-around entertainer.

I could not believe that someone I had admired since I was a child was going to be sitting right in front of me at the Saroyan Theater in Fresno, California hours before taking the stage.

Hines took a break from rehearsal, smoothly walked over to 2 chairs set up on the stage where I was waiting. I had no idea what to expect. To me, he was a mega star. I had watched him tap dance and act for years. I will never forget the moment he greeted me with a big bright smile and firm handshake, as if he was just as excited to talk to me as I was to talk to him. Rocking his signature dangling left earring, we kicked off the conversation with him explaining what it was like tap dancing, singing and entertaining large crowds of people with so much ease. He mentioned he had watched American tap dancer, Steve Condos of the Condos Brothers tap dance team.

"Sometimes he got out on stage and started dancing and he would find himself in a zone, where he felt like he could dance forever and come up with interesting stuff. It's a great feeling. Sometimes I just get into that feeling," Hines said. "Sometimes I'm out there and I think to myself, what is it about me that I like to get out on a stage with the lights on me and a whole bunch of people in the dark staring at me?" Hines laughed. He explained that his skill was the benefit of a supportive family network. "I'm one of the fortunate people in the world. I was raised in a nuclear-loving household, and I got tremendous support and encouragement in what seems like everything I did. If I was dancing, I would get a lot of feedback for that. If I sang in the shower my mom would poke her head in the bathroom and say that sounds good. You should sing more," Hines said. "So, it seems like I was always encouraged to exercise whatever talent that seemed to come up. I think that many times I feel like I can't really take a lot of responsibility for a lot of the good things that have happened to me because I've just had so much love and support that I felt confident, and I got a lot of that from my family. I think if I had to pinpoint anything I always felt like I wanted to try something because I felt like I could do it because I was encouraged and given so much support."

Like many people trying to make it in show business, Hines said he figured out you're better off if you have multiple talents and could get income from more than one source. Therefore, he wanted to create more opportunities to work. He had no desire to be an out of work tap dancer or actor.

"I think the most difficult thing is unemployment, so acting, singing, dancing or whatever is why I wanted to be versatile. I felt like it would increase my opportunities for employment, which is what I always wanted to do, I always wanted to work," Hines said. "I felt like if I could get a chance to work then I could improve. Then maybe I could do some really good work."

It proved to be a brilliant strategy. Not only did he achieve success as one of the greatest tap dancers of all time, but he also made significant strides in the film and television industries. He made his big screen debut in Mel Brooks' *History of the World Part 1* (1981). The part was written for Richard Pryor. However, days before they were ready to start shooting the film, Pryor suffered severe burns.

He starred in *The Cotton Club* (1984), *White Nights* (1985) and *Running Scared* (1986).

In 1989, he got the thrill of his life when he was in the movie *Tap* with his mentor and idol, Sammy Davis, Jr.

"I met him (Sammy Davis, Jr.) when I was 10. Over the course of the next 30 years our paths would cross, and I idolized him. He knew I idolized him. He always treated me with such generosity, such warmth, such care."

"You know everybody, every kid has an idol. Some kid somewhere idolizes Steffie Graf, or Ken Griffey or somebody. But they don't get to spend any time with that idol. They don't have that idol put their arm around them and say you can really play. You can throw that ball. You can hit. Sammy Davis, Jr. would say that to me. He would say, 'Boy, you can dance.' That's what I wanted him to say. That's what I hoped he would say, and he would say it."

Tap would be Sammy Davis, Jr.'s last movie. When you watch the film and see the two interact on screen you could see the chemistry, the mutual admiration jumping off the screen. Watching these two legends tap dance together on the screen was like watching a master class in performing arts. "Every time he would be around me, he would give me something to hold onto. Like sometimes, something good would happen to somebody and they would say, 'Oh boy, you really made my day!' Sammy Davis, just a gesture, just for him to hold my face in his hands and say 'you know you are really talented' would make my year. For a year, I would just be feeling so good."

Hines' next big screen appearance was huge. In 1995, he was one of the characters in *Waiting to Exhale*, based on Terry McMillan's screenplay. This film was a mega hit directed by Forest Whitaker, starring Whitney Houston, Angela Bassett, Loretta Devine, Lela Rochon, Gregory Hines, Dennis Haysbert, Donald Faison, and Mykaelti Williamson.

"I play Marvin who is a widower. He's one of those guys who moves into a neighborhood, he's not looking to go out on a lot of dates, he's not looking to get a lot of phone numbers. He had a relationship where he loved a woman and she died. That's what he's looking for, a relationship. He lucks up and he moves in across the street from Gloria (Loretta Devine) who he's attracted to right away. She has a son, and he can understand some of the dynamics of her relationship with her son and it's really nice." Hines was nominated for a NAACP Image Award for Outstanding Lead Actor in a Motion Picture for his character.

The movie grossed over 14 million dollars in its opening weekend, and over 82 million dollars at the box office worldwide. The soundtrack was composed by Kenneth "Babyface" Edmonds and dropped several hits that cracked the billboard top 10 including "Exhale" (Whitney Houston), "Sitting Up in My Room" (Brandy), "Let it Flow" (Toni Braxton), and "Not Gon' Cry" (Mary J. Blige).

"It's just a terrific experience right from Forest Whitaker right on down through the cast which is just loaded with some of our finest African-American actresses and it was a different experience. The film itself, I feel, is a landmark film. It's about 4 African-American women. You know they owned that set. It was great. It was a great set to be on. Terri McMillan was there. I think everybody felt that if we could just do it right, we could do something that we could all be proud of for years to come."

Hines was in more than 40 films and kept going until his death in 2003. He starred in *The Gregory Hines Show* (1997-98), *Will and Grace* (1999-2000), and he voiced the animated character "Big Bill" on the children's program, *Little Bill* (1999-2004).

He was on Broadway. He received a Daytime Emmy award, a Tony award, and nominations for a Screen Actors Guild award and Primetime Emmy awards.

In 1986, he teamed up with R&B icon, Luther Vandross, for the song, "There is Nothing Better than Love," which hit #1 on the Billboard R&B charts. Vandross also produced a song on Hines' debut album in 1988 called "That Girl Wants to Dance With Me" that charted at #8 on Billboard's Hot 100 in the spring.

After our conversation I just remember thinking to myself *wow*. Gregory Hines is an even bigger deal than I could have ever imagined. Yet, somehow, he was pleasant, humble, down to earth and full of life. My final question for him was simple and unassuming. "Did I cover it all? Is there anything else you would like to add?" I asked. Hines' response spoke volumes and said a lot about who he was.

"I'm happy to be talking to you, my brother. I'm very impressed with you!" he said with a giant smile as he got up and looked into the camera behind me and remarked to the camera man, "Did you get the 2 shots?" As I laughed and looked back, I thanked him and said, "I am with a star." He quickly responded without missing a tap dance beat. "You're the star!" Sadly, Hines passed away in August 2003 from liver cancer in Los Angeles. He was only 57 years old. Just like his idol Sammy Davis, Jr. had inspired him with kind words, Gregory Hines had inspired and impacted me.

Chapter 5

BASKETBALL TO BUSINESS: SHAQ

"We've been going through certain things for so long, I just want to do my part."

Shaq-NBA Hall of Famer

UNCONVENTIONAL WISDOM

"Wisdom is your real name? That's a great name." That was the first thing Shaquille O'Neal said when we met for the first time on Capitol Hill. Here is an NBA legend that physically was imposing, yet soft spoken and deliberate with his words. He was over 7 feet tall and over 300 pounds. I would dare say he was the tallest person in the building on this day.

By this time, Shaq had long retired from basketball and had transitioned into one of the most successful athletes-turned-commercial pitchmen. However, at this particular meeting, he wasn't promoting basketball or any product. Despite having earned 4 NBA championships, 1 MVP, and 3 finals MVPs, as well as starring in movies (such as *Blue Chips* in 1994, *Kazaam* in 1996, and *Steel* in 1997), releasing hip hop music albums (*Shaq Diesel* in 1993, *What's Up Doc & Skillz* in 1993, and *Still Can't Stop the Reign* with Biggie in 1996), appearing in numerous commercials, and transitioning into an all-around businessman, Shaq's drive and ambition never waned after he stopped dunking a basketball. In addition to pitching numerous products, he joined TNT as a NBA studio host with Ernie Johnson, Kenny Smith, and Charles Barkley. He has also been active in the community with all kinds of initiatives.

When I talked to Shaq the first time in Washington, D.C. we spoke about the problem of college binge drinking. Binge drinking refers to the act of consuming alcohol until one reaches a state of intoxication, often characterized by initially feeling a slight buzz and then continuing to drink until heavily intoxicated. "Problem with binge drinking is kids who hang out, drive home so nothing happens. So what do you do? You do the same thing next weekend. We are not telling people to stop, we are telling people to be more responsible. There are tragic stories. It only takes one mistake for a tragic story to be told. I just wanted to promote the message," Shaq told me. "Good thing about what I'm doing is, I let them create their own campaign, it's their language. People drink for different reasons, whether it is peer pressure, grades or just want to have fun. I let them produce their own spot. I just direct the spot. We encourage you to be more responsible and more conscious."

To get educated on how to best reach a younger generation, Shaq says he is on YouTube all the time because that is how young people communicate now. "YouTube sees about 4 billion videos a day. I wanted to be behind something positive. I went to college. I understand the binge drinking language. I'm not up here trying to be a saint. I was always very responsible and very conscious because I know if I took an extra drink and made a mistake it could end my career. People should have the same mentality and same attitude," Shaq said. Life after the NBA has been great for Shaq. His business interest expanded in many different directions as a basketball commentator, commercial pitch man and business owner. One of his high-profile business moves was in the pizza business. We talked about his ownership in Papa John's Pizza and why he focused his energy into that franchise.

"It's the right thing to do. I'm a board member with Papa John's, so kudos to Rob Lynch and Jeff Smith, the new ownership and leadership. We have been going through certain things for so long, I just want to do my part."

He created the Shaq-a-Roni Pizza, which he deemed the biggest pizza in pepperoni pizza history. For every pizza sold, 1 dollar goes to the Boys and Girls Club, the United Negro College Fund, and to help fight COVID and social injustices.

In 1999, Papa John's owner, John Schnatter, was accused of stalking and groping a woman. He claimed it was an extortion attempt that ended with a confidential settlement. In 2009, he was accused of sexual misconduct involving a 24-year-old female marketing employee resulting in a confidential settlement. He also blamed slumping sales on the NFL around the national anthem. That sparked controversy when racist groups declared Papa John's their official pizza.

Then, in 2018, Schnatter used the n-word on a conference call in May. During that call, he was asked how he would distance himself from racist groups online. He said, "Colonel Sanders called blacks, n---s" and said he never faced public backlash. He also, on the same call, talked about growing up in Indiana where people used to drag African Americans from trucks until they died. The company (Laundry Services Marketing Agency), that he was on the call with terminated their contract with Papa John's. Schnatter confirmed the story once it got out and issued an apology before he resigned as chairman shortly afterwards.

All of this created an avenue for the NBA Hall of Famer to step into the troubled franchise in 2019 as the first African American board member, brand ambassador and part owner of 9 franchises.

"I received a lot of flak. Once people understood the business side of it, they thought I was going in after the guy who said what he said," Shaq recalled. "When I came in, it was definitely new leadership that I trusted. I met with Jeff Smith and his family and said, "'I would love to come on, would love to be a franchisee and I would love to be on the board. I look at the way your company is set up now; you've never had an African American on the board. We love pizza and pizza loves everybody. We want to include everyone. We do not want to leave anyone out. It's 2020 and we want everyone to be a little more together.'"

Initially, Shaq appeared in TV commercials, as part of his 3 year, 8 million dollar ambassador deal.

He has several franchises in different locations throughout the country. He has earned close to 300 million dollars during his 19 year career. He says he is just as excited about being a successful businessman and making a difference.

Chapter 6

PLAYING WITH PRINCE: PRINCE'S BAND THE REVOLUTION

"He had that vision early and he was so forward thinking, he came to us and said we are going to make a movie. We are like what?"

Bobby Z

When I was growing up, Friday Night Videos on NBC held significant importance as it showcased the top music videos of the era. Among the artists frequently featured in heavy rotation was my personal favorite, Prince.

He played all his instruments, wrote and produced all his music and was a creative genius. His style was a combination of Little Richard, James Brown and Jimmy Hendrix who pushed the boundaries and limitations in music and style. I was so excited to get to see him in the summer in Las Vegas at his club, 3121. I was on my way to a journalism conference in August 2007 and was ready to cross this off my bucket list. Then just like that, in the spring of 2007, Prince concluded his residency in Vegas, dashing my hopes of ever witnessing his live performance.

In 2017, I would get the honor and thrill of talking with members of Prince's band, The Revolution. This wasn't just any band, they were an important part of the Prince legacy.

When they came in for the interview, they looked just like they did in their prime. Each one looked like they were ready to go on stage and break out any number of hit songs.

Prince started creating the tour/studio band, The Revolution, in 1979. It was the birth of the Minneapolis sound that crossed over all genres of music. Before they would officially be named, there were several changes to the members. Andre Cymone left in 1981 after the Dirty Mind Tour and was replaced by Mark Brown (stage name, BrownMark). Dez Dickerson left after the 1999 Tour and was replaced by Lisa's friend, Wendy Melvoin.

At this point, with all members in position, the Prince and the Revolution lineup included BrownMark on bass, Matt "Doctor" Fink on keyboards, Bobby Z. on drums and percussion, Wendy on guitar and bass, and Lisa on keyboards and piano. Before we went any further with the conversation, I really wanted to know more about 2 names: Doctor Fink and BrownMark.

I asked Doctor Fink about the doctor outfit.

"The band needed healthcare," Doctor Fink joked, followed by laughter from the band. "We needed someone to look after us," Lisa said. "I fulfilled that role; I still continue to take the pulse of the band," Fink said, while Bobby Z. picked up the stethoscope and checked his own heart. Now I knew I was about to get the real story. "Actually, back in the day we were on tour and I was needing to change up. I had a different outfit; black and white prison stripes. The headline act, Rick James, was wearing something similar to what I had on. So Prince came to me and requested that I change into a different outfit. We were just talking about it. He asked, 'What were your other choices?' I said, 'A guy in a doctor suit.' He says, 'That's it!'" "They went to the hospital and got one," Bobby Z. joked. "We went to the uniform shop and got one; a place in Chicago and got some scrubs," Bobby Z. said.

So, my next question was the reversal of Mark Brown's name. "One day in rehearsal, he is a practical joker, he cracks jokes. One day he says, 'I am the only brown one in the group. You are Brown Mark.'"

In 1982, the band worked with Prince on his 5th album, *1999*, featuring the chart-topping hits, "Little Red Corvette" and "1999." This is the last time Dez Dickerson would be a part of the group. At this point, they were not given any credit on the album by name.

"Prince, he did something very clever. In the 70's he was able to straddle the punk scene, the funk scene in a way a black artist hadn't done up until that point. So, by the time *1999* (the album) hit, there were some crossover hits with 'Little Red Corvette' and '1999' that sort of opened the way to this sort of culmination of his influences. When this band was formed, we all came with separate identities, separate influences, that he would actually pull from," Wendy said. "It was his own kind of dream sound from that. That is how this whole sound came up for 'Purple Rain.'"

The Revolution became officially recognized in 1984 with the iconic album and movie, *Purple Rain*. It was Prince's acting debut. The film featured first time actors, Apollonia as his love interest, and Morris Day as his music rival. Prince had created and produced music for both. Apollonia was lead singer with Apollonia 6 and Day was lead for The Time.

"I had no expectations. I had never done anything like that. I had never done television or film. It was an innocent effort," Morris told me during our conversation. "I was just doing what I had to do and it worked."

All the band members of the Revolution were in the movie. They performed and had speaking parts throughout the film.

"It was lots of fun!" Bobby Z. remembered. "We had a great time."

Purple Rain grossed more than 70 million dollars worldwide. The film won an Academy Award for Best Original Song Score.

"It was a total dream experience. Being musicians, I don't think we really dreamed about acting and sitting in my trailer waiting for my scene," Lisa recalled. The Library of Congress selected the musical motion picture film in 2019 for preservation in the National Film Registry. They described it as being culturally, historically and aesthetically significant.

"It was Prince's vision," Bobby Z. said. "He had that vision early and he was so forward thinking, he came to us and said we are going to make a movie. We are like, 'what,'" Bobby Z. said. "He had these visionary moments where he would fulfill the songs. He wrote the songs. That is what makes "Purple Rain"...His brilliance."

The *Purple Rain* soundtrack featured hits, "When Doves Cry" and "Let's Go Crazy," both of which topped the US charts. The title track, *Purple Rain*, hit number 2 on the charts. The soundtrack was certified 13 times platinum by the Recording Industry Association of America. The album has sold more than 25 million copies worldwide.

Together, Prince and the Revolution created 6 top 10 singles with 3 number 1 Billboard songs, "Let's Go Crazy," "When Doves Cry," and "Kiss." They won 3 Grammy awards together.

"He was rough. He taught us a work ethic I don't think we would have gotten in the best university, the university of purple perfection," BrownMark remembered.

The next collaboration was the number 1 album in 1985, *Around the World in a Day*.

Prince disbanded the Revolution in 1986 after their tour for the *Parade* album (soundtrack for *Under the Cherry Moon*).

It was a bitter breakup for the band due to several philosophical differences with Prince.

"For some of us there was an ambivalence to it, we knew there was an end. When it came down to distilling the reasons why he wanted to let the band go, it made perfect sense," Wendy said. "He was spending all this time with 5 million projects at once. He was giving us all a little bit more, saying "Just finish it. I'm too busy." I think by the time we were done with the *Parade* tour, we had released *Around the World in a Day*, there were other records in the vault. I think it was his way of saying this comet has just got to go," Bobby Z. said. "I am surprised he shared as much as he did with us. He started out as a solo artist. No one was more incredible on instruments than Prince making all those early albums by himself 10 glorious years. He was probably just needing to return to himself. We drove him a little crazy," Bobby Z. joked.

Following Prince's sudden death in 2016, The Revolution reunited for the first time in decades and embarked on a tour.

"It was a shock, a major shock. We called each other immediately. It's a tremendous loss the world is feeling really," Bobby Z. said.

"We are just going to stick to the stuff we were involved in. Bring it back to the fans. Deal with the grief we are all going through," Wendy said.

"He taught us to be a tight group. We hadn't seen each other for almost 20 years. We got back together in 2003. We sound like we never departed. That lesson sticks with us," BrownMark recalled. Prince and The Revolution together created musical magic. An entirely new sound that blended funk, pop, rock, jazz and everything in between. It was a special moment that had never been seen before. I would describe what they accomplished as a purple supernova passing through the musical universe that ended quickly. But there is no doubt the impact this group had on music will never be forgotten.

Chapter 7

MARVELOUS: THE RUSSO BROTHERS

"We do a lot of things that have personal meaning to us. He and I have been on a journey for 25 years as filmmakers."

Joe Russo

UNCONVENTIONAL WISDOM

It was a brilliant cinematic concept and also an original idea at the time. Take dozens of book characters from Stan Lee's Marvel comic books and adapt them to the big screen in the Marvel Cinematic Universe. First in a series of individual stories, then slowly weaving them all together into the next story and the next one. Eventually bringing all the characters together in a culmination of more than a decade of stories wrapped into one giant finale.

It was masterfully done. It was seamlessly weaved together. Keep in mind these movies were not made in chronological order. Here is the list of movies in chronological order based on the storyline.

Captain America: The First Avenger (2011), *Captain Marvel* (2019), *Iron Man* (2008), *Iron Man 2* (2010), *The Incredible Hulk* (2008), *Thor* (2011), *The Avengers* (2012), *Thor: The Dark World* (2013), *Iron Man 3* (2013), *Captain America: The Winter Soldier* (2014), *Guardians of the Galaxy* (2014), *Guardians of the Galaxy Vol. 2* (2017), *Avengers: Age of Ultron* (2015), *Ant-Man* (2015), *Captain America: Civil War* (2016), *Black Widow* (2021), *Black Panther* (2017), *Spider-Man: Homecoming* (2017), *Doctor Strange* (2016), *Thor: Ragnarok* (2017), *Ant-Man and Wasp* (2018), *Avengers: Infinity War* (2018), *Avengers: End Game* (2019).

This would make it challenging for any filmmaker to wrap it all up and make it all make sense. Here is where The Russo Brothers, Anthony and Joe, come in.

"It represents a section of our lives. It's a 7-year commitment," said Joe Russo.

They were tasked with bringing 25 years of Marvel movies to a closure with 4 of the films; *Captain America: The Winter Soldier, Captain America: Civil War, Avengers: Infinity War and Avengers: Endgame.*

"These are really difficult movies to make. The two most expensive movies ever made, shot back-to-back over the course of one year. We were literally shooting straight for one year," stated Joe Russo.

The Russo brothers were known for their work on the quirky TV comedy *Arrested Development* that ran from 2003-2005. But that was television. So how did they jump into the Marvel Cinematic Universe and juggle all these storylines and characters?

"This movie has a very special place with us in the work we have done for Marvel," Anthony Russo said.

One of the things the Russo brothers say they like to do is to get the general reaction of the audience. They do this by going into the theater and sitting in the crowd while the movie is playing.

"When you're in a theater, especially on a film like this, you hear a vocal response and people are clapping and cheering. It's just the energy! We grew up fans. We grew up with these stories we wanted to see brought to life. To be able to share that with other fans is one of the most special experiences around," Joe said.

As you watch these movies, you start to recognize how each one leads to the next. All the characters, in some way, are connected to one another. My question to the filmmakers is how do you manage all these stories and characters? How do you keep all these big-name stars/actors satisfied with screen time?

"This is something that we learned when we were developing *Captain America: Civil War*. That was the first Marvel movie we did that really had a large ensemble. What we learned was, it doesn't matter how much screen time a character has, it's what you do with it. The lesson in that movie came from characters like Spider-Man or Ant-Man who had very little screen time in that film, but they left a really big impression on the audience. For Joe and me, it was thinking of what we could do with these characters. How can we surprise audiences with what the characters are doing? How do we bring a very memorable moment to the audience by the character's appearance?" said Anthony.

"We do a lot of things that have personal meaning to us. He and I have been on a journey for 25 years as filmmakers. It started with me as an actor before I became a director. Every now and then I pop in and take a cameo under a pseudonym. My acting name is 'Go Z Actor!'"

"*Avengers: End Game* was by definition, the end of a near decade run with Marvel. It was the coup de grâce in the series. Basically, it all came down to a big clash between the good guys and bad guys," Joe said.

"The entire run of the Marvel movies was intended to be the culmination of the over 10-year, 22 movie run. We had the great benefit of this movie building on a lot of the emotional capital people have invested in the movies over the years and all these characters. The fact that the movie is taking on a special importance to people is a testament to the fact that it is speaking to this long road we have been on together," Anthony said.

After finishing up a 7-year commitment to Marvel movies, you have to wonder what's next for the brothers. How can they match the energy and excitement they created in the superhero genre?

"We have a company called AGBO. We have our own studio. We have raised a bunch of money. Steven Soderberg is an amazing filmmaker who discovered us 2 decades ago and we wouldn't be sitting here without him," Joe said.

"We got a movie we are going to go shoot with Tom Holland. It's called *Cherry* and it's based on the book. It's about a paramedic who gets hooked on heroin as a way to deal with life. It's tragic and about the opioid epidemic."

The Russo brothers created a storytelling style that departed from the traditional comic book stories. They added creativity, some grit, some edge, some conflict, some emotion, lots of action and perfectly connected it all together for an epic big finish. It's a new standard in telling stories on the big screen and managing dozens of characters and connections over an extended period of time.

What the Russo brothers achieved with the Marvel Cinematic Universe was truly magnificent.

Chapter 8

PITCH PERFECT: LESLIE JORDAN

"I'm going to come out. I'm going to tell all the boys that teased me and made fun of me, you can kiss my rich butt!"

Leslie Jordan-Actor

He may have been small in stature but he was big in laughter and personality. Comedian and actor Leslie Jordan is best known from the TV show *Will and Grace* (NBC) where he portrayed the character, Beverly Leslie. That role earned him an Emmy award for Best Guest Actor in a Comedy Series.

I talked to Jordan on June 10, 2016, as he was Grand Marshall of the Capital Pride Parade.

Jordan had also been asked to throw out the first pitch at the Washington Nationals baseball game on June 14, LGBTQ night.

He admitted that he had never thrown a baseball in his life. The thought of him standing on the mound at a Major League Baseball game in front of thousands of people scared him to death. The last thing he wanted to do was to make a fool of himself. That's where I came in. After a brief conversation, Jordan wanted me to teach him how to throw a baseball. He had been told that I had thrown out the first pitch at a Nationals game before and that at one point, I coached a little league baseball team (use the term "coach" extremely lightly).

Jordan, TV host Ross Matthews (also a guest on our show that day), and I went outside in the lot to practice. Jordan, always the entertainer, started doing cheerleader jumps to warm up. "If I get this pitch across the mound I'm going to do a Herkie! He is the father of modern cheerleading. He was married with 5 children."

"Have you done this before?" Ross Matthews asked Jordan. "Do you know how?" Jordan responded. "This is all I know. There cannot be any woman noises." Jordan, wearing a sear sucker suit, then winded up and went through a series of motions resembling a real pitcher. His first pitch to Ross Matthews was about 20 feet high and to the left. "How was that?" Jordan asked. "A little high, but that's ok. You get 3." Jordan responded with his usual self-deprecating hilarity. "I do not care about that. Did I come off like a sissy?" That comment drew the ire of Ross Matthews. I had to keep it on track by redirecting the conversation to pitching. "You look like a baseball pitcher. Let's try one more time." For Jordan's second wind up pitch, he dropped the ball. Once he recovered, he tossed it high and to the right. He then pretended his arm was injured. "Like I tell the kids, you have to own the pitch. Own it. If you make a bad pitch it's ok," I remarked. He then unbuttoned the seersucker jacket, stretched, and got ready, again, proclaiming that he was going to wear a Bryce Harper jersey when he threw out the pitch. His third pitch was down the center to the right, which was much better. He proceeded to jump up and down with his cheerleader moves, exchanging high fives. Matthews then took the ball to pitch to Jordan. My only concern was nobody getting hit in the face with the ball. "I'm feeling so *'A League of Their Own'* right now," Matthews proclaimed, before tossing the ball that bounced off the ground and into Jordan's glove. He caught the ball off the bounce, then once again launched into his cheerleader jumps in his full suit. Leslie then reminded everybody watching about the upcoming parade where he was serving as Grand Marshall. "I'm going to come out, I'm going to tell all the boys that teased me and made fun of me, 'you can kiss my rich butt!'"

Jordan mentioned some of this adventure in his 2020 autobiography, *"How Y'all Doing? Misadventures and Mischief from a Life Well Lived."* In one of his last chapters of the book, *My Last First Pitch,* he talked very kindly about the experience of me teaching him how to throw out a first pitch. He mentioned how he loved my name, especially when he found out Wisdom was my father's name that had been passed down 3 generations. He was impressed that it was my son's name too! In the chapter, Jordan talked about the moment that calmed his nerves and he knew he would not make a fool of himself when he threw out the first pitch. Just like the script out of the movie, Jordan stepped onto the mound and launched his ceremonial pitch over home plate. He admitted that he didn't even see it, but heard the crowd roar. He says it was a huge success and he was proud.

The Chattanooga native had also become an Instagram star during the Covid-19 pandemic in 2020, gaining 5.8 million followers with his comical videos. In 2021, he returned to television on the FOX series, *Call Me Kat*.

Sadly, the comedian died in a car crash in October 2022. He was 67.

Jordan left behind a legacy of laughter, resilience and overcoming. He was an actor, comedian, and LGBTQ advocate who found his voice and gave a voice to others. His style of humor and his larger-than-life personality will never be forgotten.

The pitch was a moment for Jordan, so much so that he detailed it in his book and remembered details about me! It was a humbling experience. You never know how the smallest interactions will impact a person's life.

CHAPTER 9

NEW EDITION'S NEW ADDITION: RALPH TRESVANT & JOHNNY GILL

"There was now a voice that God sent that understood what he was going through and what he was dealing with."

Johnny Gill

Growing up can be a pain. You're not a man until you come of age. That's the very first line of the New Edition song *"Boys to Men."* It is a line that you could say defines the New Edition journey. The most fascinating part of the ups and downs of this R&B supergroup is having a strong lead singer in Ralph Tresvant, then bringing in another strong voice to share the spotlight. It sounds like a recipe for some *N.E. Heartbreak*.

In 1987, solo star, Johnny Gill, of Washington, D.C. became the 6th member of New Edition. Gill's deep voice was added to the group to give them a more mature sound with super producers Jimmy Jam and Terry Lewis working on the album, *Heart Break*. Original member, Michael Bivins, recruited Gill to join the group after Bobby Brown was voted out. Lead singer, Ralph Tresvant, was rumored to be doing a solo project. Tresvant ended up staying with the group and pushing back his solo project. This could have been a recipe for disaster. Afterall, this group had dealt with Bobby Brown and his drama for years. When I got a chance to talk to Gill and Tresvant, I wanted to know how this worked. How did they bring in a lead vocalist to a successful group that already had a lead vocalist?

"People who don't know God, when God has a plan, there is destiny. We don't even know sometimes what we are going through. Why are we going through it and what's at the end of it when it's all said and done," Gill remarked. He had started his solo career at the age of 16. His first solo album *Perfect Combination* was with his good friend Stacy Lattisaw, who was already a solo star. In 1985, he dropped his second album, *Chemistry*. So joining a popular group could have been an awkward situation with Ralph. "It started from day one. We started figuring out who and why I was here. All the other things that took place. God was obviously putting things in place for where we are today. Knowing the road we were going to travel; Only He knows the outcome."

"Ralph and I endured that tumultuous period together. Through the recording process, we began to forge a deeper connection and realized we had so much in common. There was now a voice that God sent that understood what he was going through. That is ultimately what I think happened. We just connected. We became brothers. Nothing can tear us apart."

The album was a massive success. The two worked together like hand and glove. That album had charting hits like, "Can You Stand the Rain," "N.E. Heartbreak," "If It Isn't Love," and "Boys to Men" (with Gill on lead vocals).

Gill released his third solo album in 1990, collaborating with producers Jam and Lewis, as well as the producing duo of L.A Reid and Babyface. The album featured hits such as "My, My, My," "Rub You the Right Way," "Wrap My Body Tight," and "Fairweather Friend."

"I learned you put those guys together, they are some of the greatest producers to ever do it. It has been a blessing just to be able to have the opportunity to work with them. We are all friends. I've had such an incredible run. It's been unbelievable."

His other solo albums included *Provocative* in 1993 and *Let's Get the Mood Right* in 1996. Additionally, he contributed tracks such as, "There You Go" on the *Boomerang* soundtrack and "I'm Still Waiting" for the *New Jack City* soundtrack. In 1997, he formed the successful trio, LSG, with Gerald LeVert and Keith Sweat, releasing a platinum debut album titled *Levert, Sweat, Gill*.

Ralph did kick off his first successful solo project, also working with producers Jam & Lewis in 1990. The double platinum album title, *Ralph Tresvant*, had his biggest hit to date with the lead single "Sensitivity" that spent 2 weeks at #1 on the U.S charts.

"'Sensitivity' is my favorite solo record. As an individual, that song kind of spoke to a part of me I didn't know was there. I never put out a song like 'Sensitivity' or put myself in a class that way."

"After spending time with Jimmy Jam and Terry Lewis in Minneapolis, which is where they usually record stuff, they would spend time with you, get to know you; then all of a sudden, these songs come out that seem to reflect you." 'Sensitivity' is one of those songs that came out of nowhere. I didn't think that was something I was giving off but apparently I have a sensitive side!"

"That song 'Sensitivity,' and all the songs on that album were inspired by Marvin Gaye, one of my favorite artists. Between Marvin Gaye and Micheal Jackson, I listened to a lot of Stevie Wonder growing up. That's my father's favorite artist. So, the influence of Marvin Gaye came out in that song."

His list of solo songs also included, "Do What I Gotta Do" and "Stone Cold Gentleman." He also had songs on the *Mo' Money* ("Money Can't Buy You Love"), *The Preacher's Wife* ("Somebody Bigger than You and I"), and *House Party 2* ("Rated R" and "Yo, Baby, Yo!") soundtracks. One of my favorites, the Marvin Gaye infused "Who's the Mack."

"That's who I was trying to be. That's who I thought I was when I was with Jam and Lewis. They came out with Mr. Sensitivity. They represent all sides of me. I really enjoyed doing the video for 'Who's the Mack.' It was one of those videos where I got to wear a lot of different hats and outfits. I was like a double agent type."

Ralph also did some acting on the side making appearances in TV shows and movies with New Edition. He even took the stage acting in plays on occassion.

"I've been through all these places doing stage plays. Some acting roles in some movies and plan on doing more. I will lend my talents to wherever they are needed. I'm just moving around now."

He is also listed in the credits in the 2014 movie, *Get On Up*, as the legendary singer Sam Cooke. However, Tresvant told me, he was never, in any way, connected to the movie. "You know what's funny, I got billed for that. I was even in the movie credits. I saw my name. But I've never played Sam Cooke before in my life! It was a James Brown movie. I was like '*wow*'. I would like to see myself in the movie. I was never in the scene. Never contacted by anybody. I don't know how that worked. I never tried to find out. I was pleasantly shocked I got credit for something I never did. I wish I had got the check."

The Tresvant/Sam Cooke movie credits remains a mystery. What is not a mystery is that Gill and Tresvant continue their unlikely brotherhood. Tresvant made a guest appearance on Gill's 8th solo album, *Game Changer*.

"It's a blessing. I've had many number ones but to debut number 3 after 37 years of doing this, I am truly blessed," Gill said. "I just wanted to make sure, as a musician, it gave me a chance to stretch out a little bit. This album has Carlos Santana, Sheila E., Kevon Edmonds, and Ralph Tresvant on the single "Perfect," Gill said. "He (Tresvant) did the hook on 'Perfect' for me. Now, his new single, I did the hook on his called, 'All Mine.'"

In 2023, Tresvant added another accomplishment to his amazing career, becoming the radio host for "Love and R & B" with Radio One. It is the network's longest running syndicated night show on Radio One stations all over the country.

Just like the lyrics in the song "Boys To Men," these 2 legends keep learning, keep growing.

Chapter 10

ONE NIGHT IN COLLEGE PARK: THE TEXAS WESTERN GAME

"Society's eyes opened that night and began to think that we need to change. Basketball needs to change."

Nevel Shed-Texas Western Player

One of the defining moments in college basketball history happened in College Park, Maryland in 1966. The men's NCAA championship game was played at Cole Field House on the University of Maryland campus. What was so different about this March game? For the first time in the history of the game, an all-black starting 5 took the floor on the national stage. The Kentucky Wildcats, one of the dominant programs during that time, were led by coach Adolph Rupp. Texas Western (now UTEP) was coached by Don "The Bear" Haskins. Five white players from Kentucky against five black players from Texas Western.

In January of 2006, 40 years after that historic game, I had a chance to talk to some of the Texas Western players who played that night.

Nevel Shed was a 6-foot-8 junior on that team that was 23-1 that season. "You look at it as being the best playing the best," Shed said. The players say you were always aware of all the typical, negative racial stereotypes.

"It was leadership; we couldn't work under pressure. We could barely spell our names. We couldn't follow orders," Shed recalled. "We went through the same thing everybody else went through being people of color," Willie Worsley said. "We had people who didn't appreciate color. There were times when you didn't know our first name. Our last name was always 'boy.' First name was whatever they put in front of it," the sophomore starting guard told me. I also talked with Jerry Armstrong, their white teammate coming off the bench for Texas Western. "It was amazing some of the things they dealt with. But they were gentlemen. They dealt with it in gentlemanly ways."

I spoke with Jerry Bechtle who was a Maryland Terps basketball guard a few years before that game. He explained what the landscape looked like back then. "I think if you look at the teams, George Washington, Navy, Georgetown, there were no minority players back then. From the east coast perspective, Cole Field House was historic. It really was," Bechtle said. At the time there were no black players in the ACC (Atlantic Coast Conference) where the Maryland Terps played. The conference was desegregated in 1963 with football, and basketball in 1964. "We played a few teams in the Midwest, Indiana, Northwestern. I have to say, that was our first exposure at Maryland playing against a black athlete," said Bechtle. "Everything changed March 19, 1966 at Cole Field House on Maryland's campus when 5 black starters took the court for an NCAA championship game."

With the basketball world watching, Texas Western shocked the nation beating Kentucky 72-65. "They say we shall overcome. Well, we overcame that night," said sophomore Willie Cager.

It wasn't just a victory for Texas Western that night or that season. That basketball game was a game changer moving forward in college athletics. Recruiting changed all over the south. Historically none of the southern schools recruited black players. "There were so many other basketball players back then who wanted the chance. We were blessed with having the chance," Nevel Shed recalled. "Society's eyes opened that night and began to think that we need to change. Basketball needs to change." Kentucky had been an all-white program until 1969. The Southeastern Conference, where Kentucky played, had their first black basketball player in 1967.

Nashville native, Perry Wallace, integrated the SEC when he played for Vanderbilt University that year. Godfrey Dillard from Detroit was also a member of the team. The SEC was the last basketball conference to integrate when Wallace started the season opener against SMU.

In February 2006, President George Bush invited the team to the White House to be recognized for the barriers they broke by overcoming the odds in 1966. In 2007, the team was inducted into the Naismith Memorial Basketball Hall of Fame.

"Forty years late, but forty years right on time," Nevel Shed told me with a giant smile on his face. "I'll take it! You got to get your props," Willie Cager said. Texas Western coach Don Haskins was not able to make the trip to Washington because of health issues.

The journey of this team is detailed in the 2006 movie *Glory Road*. The win by Texas Western changed the landscape of college sports. Five black starters. One huge win. Decades of racial bias and stereotypes in college basketball started to erode after that one season and one magical night in College Park, Maryland.

Chapter 11

AIR JORDAN'S LAST FLIGHT: A MOMENT WITH JORDAN

"It is my last home game in Washington and it's something I will treasure."

　　　Michael Jordan-NBA Hall of Famer

In 2003, Michael Jordan was in his final season with the Washington Wizards. The morning of Monday, April 15, the greatest basketball player to ever walk the planet was about to walk out of his final practice at what was then called the MCI Center in downtown Washington, D.C. I was with a group of reporters waiting for Air Jordan to come out of the locker room and give his last home pre-game interviews with the media hours before his last home game against the New York Knicks.

I remember us standing in the hallway of the building anxiously waiting for the team's morning shootaround to end. One by one, the players came out of the locker room. At one point, NBA legend Pat Ewing (assistant coach at the time) walked through the crowd of media shaking his head with a smirk on his face. More players walked out, and still no sign of Jordan. Coach Doug Collins eventually came out and talked to the press reflecting on the Jordan years. Collins talked about how he loved to talk basketball with Jordan because he was a genius. After that conversation with Collins, the waiting game continued in the hall. Then, after about 45 minutes, Jordan emerged in the hallway sporting his all-white Jordan jogging suit with the red Jordan logo, a white Air Jordan hat (looked like a soft brim bucket hat) and his trademark Jordan shoes. He was on his phone at the time, so he did not immediately come over to address us. He stood alone at the end of the hall, finishing his phone conversation. Five minutes later, Jordan hung up the phone, approached us, leaned against the wall, and patiently waited for questions.

"It is my last home game in Washington and it's something I will treasure. I woke up this morning and thought there was a certain feeling I should be feeling." Jordan said that it was a normal day, nothing out of the ordinary. He just had breakfast and coffee and went about his normal routine.

This was a monumental moment for Washington and the NBA. Jordan had joined Washington in the front office after his retirement as President of Basketball Operations, working with team owner, Abe Pollin. From January 2000 through October 2001, Jordan would make the decisions when it came to the team roster.

In October, he decided to come out of retirement for the 3rd time and wear the red, white, and blue of the Wizards. It was an improbable move considering 5 years before, he had won his 6th NBA Championship with the Chicago Bulls, defeating the Utah Jazz with one of the most iconic final shots in the history of the game.

Once he returned to the court, the eyes of the basketball world would turn to Washington to see if the 38-year-old legend could still hold up to the rigorous NBA schedule. Financially, it was a huge success for the team. During his 2 seasons of his final comeback, the team had 82 consecutive sellouts. Every home game at the MCI Center over that 2-year run sold out. This was a team that last made the playoffs in 1997 when Jordan's Bulls swept them in the first round. Washington had jumped into the national broadcast spotlight because fans and viewers were fascinated to see basketball greatness on his last run.

I asked him about the impact he had on the team.

"There has been some improvement because we are not strapped financially," Jordan said. "If I had a chance to come back for another team, I would not have come back to a veteran team because they did not need me to come back. I felt like there was a need to come back and teach."

Despite the realization that at the age of 40, his on-court journey had reached its conclusion, was the greatest basketball player ever truly prepared to officially retire this time?

"This is definitely it. With the Bulls, it was not my choice. If Phil would have stayed, I would have stayed. I did not want to play for a rebuilding project. This time it is my choice."

It was not a perfect ending for Jordan who finished with 21 points and 8 rebounds. The Knicks ended up beating Washington 93-79 on "Jordan Appreciation Night." He left the game to a monstrous ovation that lasted the final 2 minutes of the game. At age 40, Jordan was not able to get the Wizards to the playoffs in either of his 2 seasons. The Wizards were no longer going to be the league's biggest draw. In those 2 seasons, franchise profits increased by an estimated 10 million dollars each season.

The tables were set now for Jordan to negotiate his return to the front office with Washington owner, Abe Pollin. Somehow those meetings/negotiations got derailed fast and ended in a shouting match between the 2 men. In their last meeting, Pollin decided not to rehire Jordan and go in a "different direction." Jordan was outraged about what had been promised to him. Security working in the building at the time recalled hearing the 2 men arguing, and Jordan storming out of the office yelling some words that cannot be repeated. They recall him heading directly to the garage, getting in his convertible Mercedes and speeding out of the MCI Center 3 weeks after taking off the Wizards jersey.

Jordan had taken a below-market salary to play for a team that he put back in the limelight nationally and packed the arena. Then, when it was time for him to go back to the front office, the team said no thanks. Abe Pollin released a statement. "I do believe Michael's desire to win and be successful is unquestioned. In the end… Ted Leonsis and I felt that this franchise should move in a different direction."

Jordan also released a statement. "I am shocked by this decision, and the callous refusal to offer me any justification for it." It was the end of Jordan's time with the Wizards, but in 2010, he purchased the Charlotte Bobcats for 275 million dollars. He eventually changed the name of the team back to the Charlotte Hornets (the original name of Charlotte's team). Thirteen years later, he sold his majority share of the team for 3 billion dollars, thereby concluding his tenure as the sole African-American majority owner in the NBA, NFL, or MLB. In a press release, Jordan said, "The opportunity to be the majority owner of the Charlotte Hornets in my home state of North Carolina for the last 13 years has been a tremendous honor." In the end, Jordan got his team in his home state and made history becoming the first and only African-American franchise owner in the big 3 American sports.

Chapter 12

REALITY: NENE LEAKES

"You got to have thick skin. You have to know who you are, because if you step into reality TV, they will tell you that you are horrible."

NeNe Leakes-Reality TV Star

NeNe Leakes is the ultimate reality TV original. In 2008, she became the superstar of Bravo Television's *Real Housewives of Atlanta*. She was an original cast member and a main character for the first 7 seasons. In 2015, she left the franchise but was in season 8 as a featured guest. She eventually came back to the show for seasons 10-12 from 2017-2020.

"It is very difficult. You got to have thick skin. You have to know who you are, because if you step into reality TV, they will tell you that you're horrible. If you do not know who you are, you will be jacked up. For a lot of women who have come and gone, they were the difficult ones and did not have staying power. You got to know why you are in it. When you are in it, they talk about your 15 minutes of fame, you got to know how to make that thang jump off! I launched mine into years," Leakes says. "I do know that people think from watching TV, I'm difficult. I can tell you this, difficult people ain't working. If you are difficult, they kick your butt out."

Leakes says she is opinionated and direct. Sometimes direct can come off as harsh. "If you want to know the truth, I'll shoot it to you straight. If I shoot it to you straight, sometimes you are like Wow. That was brutal. My heart is as big as ever; if I love you, I love you," she said. "I don't want to be difficult. But I'm always going to be the girl to tell you just like it is. That's why sometimes people ask me stuff and I don't say nothing. I know you don't want to hear what I got to say. Because I would say it straight, it will come off like that was rude. It's really just me being honest."

In 2020, Leakes made the decision to depart from reality TV and explore other opportunities, particularly focusing on furthering her acting career. Notably, she appeared as the swimming coach in Season 3 of the FOX show *Glee*. Additionally, she showcased her talents in various other endeavors including, *The Apprentice, Dancing with the Stars,* resident shows like *Cirque du Soleil: Zumanity*, Broadway's *Cinderella*, and more. Following her initial season, she co-authored a book titled, "Never Make the Same Mistake Twice."

"I started saying OMG! I want to be an actress and maybe this will be an opportunity for me to be an actress. Then low and behold Ryan Murphy called me and said we want you to be on *Glee* as Coach Roz! I ended up being on that show for almost 4 years. I had lots of opportunities to come to me. I feel like the opportunities came to me rather than me actively pursuing them. They came to me because I was real. You could talk to me, I felt like I related to the viewers, and they relate to me."

NeNe also parlayed her reality popularity into a television production company, NeNe Leakes Entertainment, a fashion line for the Home Shopping Network, and the SWAGG Boutique locations in Miami and the MGM National Harbor just outside Washington, D.C.

"I am hoping to have variety at the casino. I also want to interact with the locals with kimonos, dresses, evening gowns, swimwear… a little bit of everything. I wanted everybody to walk in and afford something. We also have a range of sizes 2-24. Everybody can come eat 2 burgers and get dressed."

Leakes, at the time, was in the D.C. area to open a pop-up boutique at the National Harbor in Maryland.

"I love fashion. I think it's a part of expressing yourself. I love to see other women look good. I feel like I have the eye to shop for other women, their body types. I shop for them more than I shop for myself. I like to see women look great. It's really that simple. During the week, I am plain Jane, sweats, and jeans."

As we came to the end of the conversation, I told the reality O-G that she was really nice for making time to talk to me. She replied, grabbing my hand in a playful way and laughing, "I am a fun girl naturally. We are having fun right now, and I didn't even have anything to drink," she spoke. "I love shopping obviously. I love to travel. I must say I do love to work. I like what I do. But I like to work." Since she brought up the subject of travel, we kept talking. Naturally I wanted to know where she likes to vacation.

"One of my favorite places to travel is Africa. I love it. It was so different to me. I really like Angola. I feel like it's very peaceful to me. My place in the states is Miami."

She then told me she wished I had a call-in option because she would really love to talk to people because she is a self-described open book.

Here is how that conversation went. "We are not on that level. That's not in the budget," I told her. "You're not? All you gotta do is have your phone, get a speaker, like these conference call numbers," she responded.

"Maybe after this, we will because of you!" I responded.

She replied, "I hope you blow up. I blew up a lot of people and got no commission."

"If I blow up, I'll pay," I shot back.

"Oh, really?" she said. "All I want is a wig and a pair of shoes. My wigs are expensive, honey. I want red bottoms, honey!"

The laughter and hilarity was coming to a close. Before she wrapped things up, she left me with a few more gems.

"You are going to do good from this. People will want to hear your show. You will have to be a straight shooter. That's the only way to get viewers. People love to hate people for that. It's a good thing. They love to hate you, your pockets get great. Just tell it like it is. People will be like I can't stand him, let me call in. That's going to be the best thing ever!"

ABOUT THE AUTHOR

Wisdom Martin is a veteran television news journalist and anchor with more than 30 years of experience covering news and sports. He started at WJSU radio then moved to television covering college football and other sports in Jackson, Mississippi (WAPT) before heading west covering news and sports in Fresno, California (KSEE). He later moved east to North Carolina where he covered news (WRAL) and both the North Carolina Tar Heels football and basketball. He also covered national news at CNN in Atlanta, before moving to Nashville, Tennessee (WKRN), as an anchor and breaking news reporter. In 2003, Wisdom moved to Washington, D.C. where he covered local and national news, including 5 presidential inaugurations. He also covered Michael Jordan's last season with the Washington Wizards, George Mason University basketball run to The Final 4, Maryland Lady Terps championship run as well as Washington Nationals return to Washington and World Series win in 2019. During his career span, he has covered a variety of stories which included the 1994 arrest and trial of Byron De La Beckwith, the convicted murderer of NAACP Field Secretary Medgar Evers, the serial bank robbers in Washington D.C., Hurricane Katrina in New Orleans, the death of Washington football star Sean Taylor, and more. His first book, "Pass Interference: The History of the Black Quarterback in the NFL" was published in 2022.

For more info go to wisdommartin.com

www.ingramcontent.com/pod-product-compliance
Lightning Source LLC
Chambersburg PA
CBHW072212070526
44585CB00015B/1310